W9-BVD-605

DRUGS AND VIOLENT CRIME

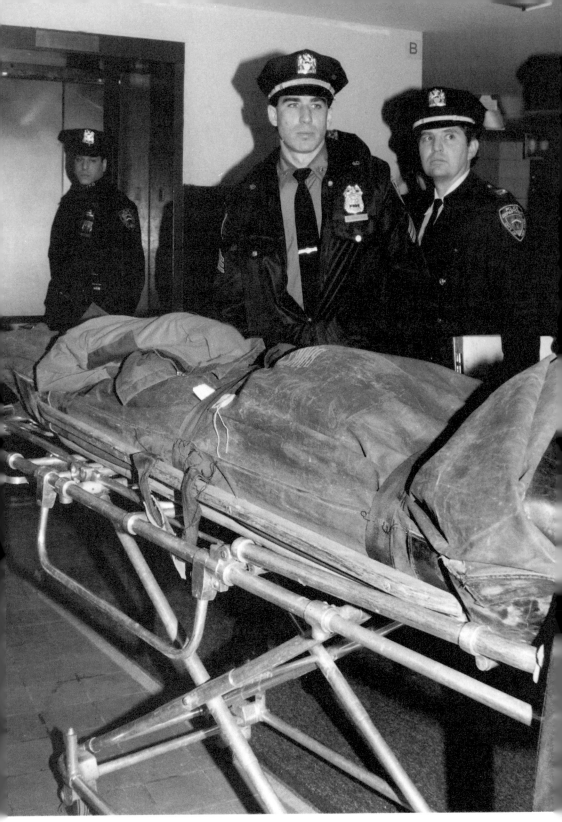

The problem of drugs and violent crime has claimed
many lives.

THE DRUG ABUSE PREVENTION LIBRARY

DRUGS AND VIOLENT CRIME

Maryann Miller

THE ROSEN PUBLISHING GROUP, INC.
NEW YORK

Published in 1996 by The Rosen Publishing Group, Inc.
29 East 21st Street, New York, NY 10010

First Edition

Library of Congress Cataloging-in-Publication Data
Miller, Maryann, 1943–
    Drugs and violent crime / Maryann Miller. — 1st ed.
      p.   cm. — (The drug abuse prevention library)
    Includes bibliographical references and index.
    Summary: Discusses the dangers associated with drugs including the connections between drugs and violent crime.
    ISBN 0-8239-2282-0
    1. Drug abuse and crime—Juvenile literature.
[1. Drug abuse and crime.   2. Violent crimes.
3. Violence.]   I. Title.   II. Series.
HV5809.5.M554   1996
364.2′4—dc20   95-26264
                                                       CIP
                                                        AC

Manufactured in the United States of America

The people pictured in this book are only models; they in no way practice or endorse the activities illustrated. Captions serve only to explain the subjects of the photographs and do not imply a connection between the real-life models and the staged situations shown. News agency photographs are exceptions.

Contents

Introduction

Stephen doesn't play ball on the street or hang out with his friends in the neighborhood. When he walks to school, he is always on guard.

Stephen lives in a neighborhood where gangs have taken over. Drug deals take place near his house. And his school has become like a prison to try to keep out the bad guys and their guns.

Someday Stephen would like to live in a place where he can feel safe, but he doesn't really expect it to happen.

Violence has become a big problem in the United States. On the average, thirteen teens are killed every day through murders, accidents, or suicides. In 1990, handguns killed ten people in Australia, twenty-two in Great Britain, and sixty-eight in Canada as compared to 10,567 in the United States. But you may be thinking, "So what? What does violence have to do with drugs?"

One theory is that the drug market often recruits teens to sell drugs, to be lookouts, or to be couriers. Drug dealers often give these teens guns to carry to protect themselves and the drugs. Other kids begin imitating them by carrying guns too.

In addition, at least 60 percent of violent crime is associated with drug use. Drug addicts commit fifteen times as many robberies and twenty times as many burglaries as criminals not on drugs.

There *is* a link between drugs and violent crime. Whether you live in an inner city or in a suburban neighborhood, many of you have either experienced it firsthand or seen it on the evening news. Drug-related violence is a growing phenomenon that is taking many victims.

This book discusses the dangers associated with drugs. When you understand the effects that drugs have on you as well as the violence involved with drugs, you can make choices for your life to keep you safer.

It can be very hard to resist pressure from friends about drugs, but it's the best option.

CHAPTER 1

The Drugs People Abuse

Marcy and Jennifer sat on the park bench, careful to stay in the shadows. It was after curfew. They didn't want to be spotted by the police car that frequently patrolled the area.

Jennifer pulled a six-pack of beer out of a paper bag. She popped one open, took a swig, and offered another to Marcy, who shook her head. "Come on," Jennifer said. "What can it hurt?"

Have you ever been in a situation like this and been tempted to give in to your friend? You may think it wouldn't hurt to try just once, but you're wrong. Even one beer can hurt you.

Beer contains alcohol, and alcohol is a

10 dangerous drug. A drug is a chemical that changes the way a person feels, thinks, or behaves. Experimenting with drugs is dangerous, even if it is just one beer. One beer can affect your judgment and make you do things that you wouldn't do if you were sober, such as getting behind the wheel of a car without a license or driving drunk. If you get into an accident, that one beer can cost you your life.

Many people think experimenting with drugs is harmless, but it is very easy to become hooked. When you first start, a little can give you a pleasant feeling, called a *high*. Gradually your body will need more and more drugs to get that same high. You will start craving it and will do just about anything to get more. This is called *addiction*. Many people develop a chemical addiction almost at once. At first a small amount of the drug satisfies them. Then their bodies demand more, and they begin to depend on it.

In addition to a physical dependency, some people form a psychological dependency. Drugs seem to block out the problems in their lives, so they continue to take drugs. But drugs don't solve problems, they only create more.

Long-term drug abuse can cause

Users usually experience depression when they crash.

several mental health problems. It can cause mental confusion, irritability, outbursts of aggression, and paranoid thinking. Many people also suffer from severe depression that can lead to suicide or attempted suicide.

Personality disorders can also develop. Paranoid psychosis is a disorder that causes feelings of persecution. The person becomes suspicious of others for no reason. Another disorder, compulsive behavior, causes nervousness and irritability.

These disorders, and others, can lead to bizarre and often violent behavior.

12 | *Legal Drugs*

When people think of drugs, they often think of illegal drugs such as cocaine or marijuana. Many people don't realize that medicines (those bought over-the-counter and those that require a doctor's prescription) and caffeine (usually found in coffee, tea, and colas) are also drugs. These are considered legal drugs.

Some drugs, such as alcohol (found in drinks such as beer, wine coolers, whiskey, and vodka) and nicotine (found in the tobacco in cigarettes and cigars), are illegal for teenagers. You must be over twenty-one to buy and drink alcohol, and over eighteen to buy and smoke tobacco.

Although both alcohol and tobacco are legal for adults, they are dangerous drugs and can cause life-long addiction.

Alcohol

Some people don't realize that alcohol is a drug—perhaps because it is legal for adults. Public intoxication and driving under the influence of alcohol (DWI or DUI) are illegal, however. So is possession and use of alcohol by those under twenty-one.

Alcohol is not immediately addictive, but it does have immediate effects. It in-

terferes with the normal workings of the
central nervous system. That's why people
stumble and slur their speech when they
are drunk.

Alcohol can make you very sick if you
drink too much. For many teens, drinking fun ends when they become violently
sick and pass out. There is also the
danger of alcohol poisoning. If you weigh
about 100 pounds and drink a whole
bottle of wine in a short period, your
body can't process all the alcohol. Because alcohol is toxic, you could go into
shock and die.

Tobacco

Tobacco contains many harmful ingredi-
ents, two of which are: nicotine (which
can damage the lungs, throat, and other
organs) and tar (which can cause cancer).
Tobacco is a stimulant which means it
speeds up the nervous system. Tobacco
can also reduce the amount of blood that
reaches the heart.

Alcohol and tobacco are sometimes
known as gateway drugs. Teens who start
abusing one or both of these two drugs
may eventually start using stronger drugs.
This often creates a cycle of addiction
that can lead to violence.

14 | *Illegal Drugs*

Drugs such as crack, marijuana, heroin, and cocaine are illegal for everyone. A person can be arrested if he or she is caught buying or using these drugs.

Stimulants

Often called "uppers," stimulants include marijuana, amphetamines, cocaine, and crack. These drugs act on the central nervous system, creating a "high," a feeling of excitement or *euphoria*. They increase a person's heart rate, blood pressure, and body temperature.

Marijuana is made from the leaves of the *Cannabis sativa* plant and is usually smoked. Tetrahydrocannabinol or THC is the chemical in the plants that gives users the high. Marijuana is also called "weed," "grass," and "pot." It can affect the user physically like a stimulant, but it can also cause hallucinations, especially if it is used in combination with another drug.

Cocaine and crack are highly addictive drugs. Both are made from coca leaves. Cocaine is a powder that is usually inhaled through the nose or injected directly into a vein. Cocaine causes different reactions in different people. Some users feel alert and overconfident

while others become confused and paranoid. Cocaine can also cause convulsions
and even death. In some cases, people
have died the first time they tried
cocaine.

Crack or "rock" is a more potent form
of cocaine. It is usually a combination of
cocaine and baking soda or ether and
comes in the form of large, white crystals.
Crack can be either smoked or melted
down and injected (freebased). It produces a very strong high which lasts only
five to ten minutes. Crack affects the user
the same way as cocaine, only faster. It
increases blood pressure, makes the heart
beat very fast, and lowers oxygen intake
in the brain. These effects might cause
the user to have a stroke or a heart
attack. The crash is very strong. The user
feels tired and extremely depressed. A
person can become hooked on crack the
first time he or she tries it.

Methamphetamine is another stimulant
which causes effects similar to those of
cocaine. On the street it is called "speed,"
"crank," "crystal," or "crystal meth."
People who use this drug often "binge"
(taking the drug to get high) then experience a "crash." During the crash they
may suffer depression, irritability, anxiety,

Barbiturates and alcohol can make a deadly combination.

and insomnia (inability to sleep). In extreme cases the drug can cause a psychosis similar to paranoid schizophrenia, a disorder marked by a false sense of greatness and hallucinations.

Barbiturates

Usually called "downers," these drugs are legally used as sleeping pills and muscle relaxants. They are also sold illegally on the streets. Barbiturates slow the body's functions and make the user feel mellow. But if bodily functions slow too much, the heart can stop.

Barbiturates are highly addictive. Addicts need more of the drug to achieve the same results. Barbiturates are especially dangerous when used together with alcohol. Both substances reduce breathing rate and lower blood pressure, which can lead to coma and death.

Narcotics

Narcotics are also called opiates. They are made from the juice of the poppy plant. Morphine, an opiate, is used legally as a painkiller, but doctors are careful when prescribing it because it is so addictive.

Heroin is another opiate. Unlike morphine, heroin is illegal. Also called "horse," heroin is injected. Heroin lowers the heart rate. The user often feels restless, drowsy, or nauseated. Although heroin produces a high that can last up to six hours, the crash that follows can last for days. Heroin, like crack, can be immediately addictive. The user needs more and more heroin to get high and satisfy the craving for the drug.

Hallucinogens

These include LSD and PCP. LSD, lysergic acid diethylamide, also known as "acid," has been used widely since the 1960s. It can cause flashbacks, wild mood swings, panic and confusion.

PCP, phencyclidine, also called "angel dust," has been around as long as LSD but became more popular in the 1970s and 1980s. PCP can produce paranoia, intense anger, and hostility. Some experts believe it causes more violent behavior than any other drug.

PCP and LSD distort reality. They can make users see and hear things that aren't there. These drugs are especially dangerous because a user can have what's known as a "bad trip," a bad experience, while on the drug. People have died in accidents that occur during bad trips.

Steroids

These are human-made, or synthetic, forms of natural hormones. Hormones are chemicals that our bodies produce naturally to control bodily activities. The male hormone testosterone controls muscle growth and height. Many athletes, especially bodybuilders, use steroids to get stronger faster. One danger of steroid use is that it can turn off the body's natural hormone system so that normal growth stops.

Other risks of taking steroids are both physical and emotional. Tommy Chaikin, a football player for the University of

Some teens develop their drug habits at an early age.

South Carolina in the early 1980s, took steroids for three years. The steroids caused high blood pressure, a heart murmur, and eventually tumors. Chaikin also became extremely aggressive. In an article in *Sports Illustrated*, Chaikin said that he became irritated over minor things. Once he started a fight with someone who accidentally bumped into him.

Another danger of steroids is depression, which can lead to suicide. Recently, an eighteen-year-old hanged himself. His parents believe the suicide was brought on by the use of steroids. They hadn't known he was using steroids. They had

20 | noticed, however, that he acted more aggressive and violent after he started bodybuilding.

Inhalants

These include a wide variety of substances including glue, gasoline, paint thinner, and ether. By sniffing the inhalant, a person gets a sort of high. Children as young as eight or nine have used inhalants.

Inhalant abuse may lead to the use of other drugs, including alcohol, marijuana, and amphetamines. It may also lead users to damage property, shoplift, and commit other crimes.

We have only mentioned some of the dangers involved with drugs. If you decide to try drugs, you risk becoming addicted. This will not only affect *your* life, but it will affect the lives of your family, friends, and everyone else around you. Drugs cause many users to become violent. This violence can occur when they need money to support their habits. An addiction to a drug can cause you to lie, steal, and event commit violent crimes. Keep this in mind before you decide to take a sip of beer or a puff of a joint.

Violence in This Society

*V*iolence among young people has become an epidemic. According to the Federal Bureau of Investigation (FBI), one in every six arrests for murder, rape, robbery, or assault is a suspect under eighteen. Too many children of this generation are born to teenage mothers who are still children themselves. These children often grow up in a single-parent home in inner-city neighborhoods controlled by drug dealers. The cycle of drugs and violent crime grows when these children follow the paths of the drug dealers.

Perhaps that reality can be best illustrated in the story of Jacob.

22 | *Jacob Gonzales, ten, and Damien Dorris, fourteen, were each born to women on welfare. Jacob lived in a crack house with his mother. He took his first drag of marijuana when he was nine. His father used to beat his mother before he was shot to death in a bar fight. Jacob saw his sister shot in the face when he was four or five. His mother first gave birth at the age of fourteen and had a total of eight children. According to court records, she drank heavily, used crack, and had even stooped to selling her children's clothes to get money for crack.*

Damien was abandoned by his father and beaten by his mother. He had dropped out of school after the seventh grade and lived with an older brother who dealt drugs. Damien eventually learned the tricks of the trade from his brother.

One August afternoon in 1993, Jacob and Damien waited in the parking lot of a bank for someone to rob. Damien owed $430 to his drug suppliers, which he had to return in twenty-four hours or risk being killed.

Elizabeth Alvarez, pregnant and the mother of three, was their victim. Jacob and Damien went up to her after she withdrew some money for her child's birthday party. When she refused to hand over the money, Damien shot and killed her at Jacob's signal.

This 1993 incident was described in a 1994 series about juvenile crime in the *New York Times* by Isabel Wilkerson.

According to the story, people wondered about Jacob's casual attitude after the crime. The reporter said that we had only to look at Jacob's past to understand.

Children like Jacob and Damien don't realize there is any other kind of life. They are only doing what they consider normal.

Many cities have become targets for drugs and violence. In some schools in Chicago, police patrol cars stand by to keep order during recess. Eighty-eight people across the city were murdered in March of 1994 alone. At the Robert Taylor Homes, a huge public housing project, more than 300 shootings occurred in a span of four days.

Drugs and violence are not only happening in cities, but also in small rural areas. Several high schools in Iowa have full-time probation officers in the school to watch over those students on parole. Specially trained dogs have been brought into schools in Blue Ridge, Arizona, Savannah, Georgia, and Emery, Utah, to sniff out drugs and guns.

24   A 1990 FBI report showed that almost one third of people convicted of robbery and burglary committed the crime to get money for drugs.

Police in Washington, DC, say that drugs are responsible for 80 percent of the murders there.

Almost half the juveniles in correctional facilities for crimes committed in 1993 acted under the influence of drugs or alcohol.

Other Types of Violence

Homicide is only one of the violent crimes associated with drug use. *Assault with a deadly weapon* is the use of a gun, knife, or other weapon to injure a person. *Simple assault* is injuring a person without a weapon.

Rape is another violent crime, as is *sexual assault*. A story in *Today* magazine (May 1994) reported an increase of violence on college campuses. Incidents of rape, sexual assault, and physical assault are increasing. Most cases are related to drinking or other drug abuse.

Domestic violence is also of growing concern. Every day in the United States three to four women are killed by their husbands. The assailant in 85 percent of

The murder trial of O. J. Simpson made many people
aware of the problem of domestic violence.

26 | these cases had prior reports of assault. The highly publicized trial of O. J. Simpson caught the attention of the nation. Simpson was accused of the brutal murders of his ex-wife, Nicole Brown Simpson, and her friend, Ron Goldman. During the trial, prosecutors presented as evidence Simpson's history of abuse toward Nicole, including her frantic 911 call and photos of her bruised and beaten. Although Simpson was acquitted of the crime of murder, the trial made millions of people worldwide aware of the problem of domestic violence.

Domestic violence has two effects. The first effect is the injury or death of the victim. The second effect is what happens to kids who are victims of, or witnesses to, domestic violence. We have seen what the constant exposure to violence did to Jacob.

A study of inmates at the federal penitentiary at San Quentin, California, supports the opinion that domestic violence promotes violent crime. Every one of the inmates who had been convicted of violent crimes had suffered family violence as a young child.

Another example of violence leading to more violence is Robert Sandifer, an

Actions of a mother can have negative effects on her child.

28 | eleven-year-old who was shot and killed in Chicago in September 1994. Sandifer, a suspect in the death of a fourteen-year-old, was gunned down by two gang members. At the time, it was thought that Sandifer was killed so he wouldn't talk about the gang's involvement in the first killing.

Sandifer never had a chance from the time he was born. He had been beaten and abused by his mother. At age three, he was taken away from his mother, and thereafter he lived either in state homes or with his grandparents. The only family he really had was his gang.

Unfortunately, his gang found him expendable.

Violence and Women

Many people are concerned about the rise in the number of women involved in violent crimes. The number of women in state and federal prisons increased from 12,331 in 1980 to 43,845 in 1990—that's an increase of 256 percent. The male prison population increased only 140 percent. The involvement in violent crimes for women under age eighteen increased by 68 percent; the increase for male youths was over 45 percent.

Many criminologists believe that female crime rates are growing because of poverty and other social factors. The number of single mothers is at an all-time high. Most of these women are young and have no means of support. The temptation to commit crimes to support their children is strong.

The percentage of women in prison for drug crimes is higher than for male inmates. The number of babies born addicted to crack also shows the high rate of drug use among women.

Another point of interest is the number of young women joining violent street gangs. This development is so new that it has not had time to affect statistics or opinions. In an article (1994) in *Scholastic*, Gini Sikes tells the chilling story of Regina. After a rival gang member shot and killed the brother of Regina's friend, Regina sought revenge. Disguising herself as a boy, she found the guy at a party bragging about the killing. Regina went up to him and said, "This is the big payback from the hood." Then she shot him twice.

Regina escaped, took off her disguise, and was never caught. The boy she shot survived. He doesn't know that a girl pulled the trigger.

30   Gangs of young women pattern themselves after the male gangs. They commit similar crimes, which range from carjacking to armed robbery. The fact that more girls are willing to take the risks of drugs and crime is seen by some experts as a real problem for the future. "Girls become mothers, and mothers influence the behavior of their offspring," says Joan McCord, a professor of criminology at Temple University.

A recent study by the Justice Department found that two-thirds of women in prison have at least one child who is under the age of eighteen. McCord believes that the actions of the mothers can have a negative effect on the children. In some cases it can even lead them into a life of crime and violence.

CHAPTER 3

How Drugs Cause Violence

*T*he cause-and-effect relationship between drugs and violence is on two levels. Violence is associated with the *use* of drugs and with the *business* of drugs.

One of the most common signs of drug use is a change in personality and behavior. For instance, Joe used to be easygoing and laid back. He started to become aggressive and unpredictable and would blow up over nothing.

That behavioral change is one of the psychological effects of drug use. A recent study in New York showed that some drugs cause users to "become excitable or irrational." Drugs can also cause users to "act out in a violent manner."

Drastic changes in a friend's behavior may indicate drug use.

Drugs can give a person the courage to commit an act of violence. By altering reality, the drugs make the person believe that the violence is not wrong. That's what happened to a young man named Frank who shot a convenience store clerk during a robbery. Frank was so high that he couldn't separate make-believe from reality. To him, what he was doing was like television or a movie. It wasn't real, so it couldn't be wrong.

Drugs can also give a person the courage to do something he or she *does* know is wrong. This is common in gang initiations. Many young gang members are terrified at having to be part of something like a drive-by shooting. They take drugs to numb the fear. Then they can do what they must to be accepted.

Drug use also causes what some experts call *economic compulsive violence*— violence that occurs while an addict is trying to get money to buy drugs. Victims are often assaulted or killed during a robbery, mugging, or burglary.

The New York police think the increase in homicides is directly related to the use of crack. The proportion of drug-related killings in New York rose from 25 percent in the early 1980s to almost 40 percent in 1988.

Drugs are also a major factor in suicides, especially among teenagers. Teen suicide has increased over 300 percent in the past twenty years. About 126 young people commit suicide every week, or one about every eighty minutes. Many of those suicides are connected with drug use.

Some young people turn to drugs to escape the difficulties of their lives. For many of them, the escape is another trap—addiction. One young woman, found dead in her car from carbon monoxide fumes, left a note written as her own version of the Twenty-Third Psalm:

34 | "King heroin is my shepherd, I shall always want . . . Surely heroin addiction shall stalk me all the days of my life and I will dwell in the house of the Damned forever."

It is obvious that a person who is having trouble coping with life will not find a solution in drugs. As we've already learned, drug use can create psychological and emotional problems. It can also push someone over the edge. Sober, a person might only think about suicide. High on some drug, that person could take the fatal step.

Not Just Illegal Drugs

Drugs commonly used to treat mental illness or emotional problems can also be harmful. Tranquilizers and antipsychotic drugs are similar to many of the illegal drugs and can cause similar psychological problems. When misused, they can also cause violent behavior or death.

According to a report in *USA Today* (May 1994), many elderly people die every day because of these drugs. This problem arises in some nursing homes where the residents are drugged to keep them quiet and manageable. The American Hospital Association reports that of the almost 11 million elderly admitted to hospitals every year, about 2 million are suffering drug reactions.

According to another report in the *Daily News* (October 1995), a growing number of children are also taking these medicines. The number of children taking Ritalin, a behavior-control drug that can be addictive, has doubled in the past five years, according to the National Institute of Mental Health. Prescriptions for antidepressants (drugs used to treat depression), such as Prozac and Zoloft, are also increasing. In 1992 alone, doctors prescribed, recommended, or administered antidepressant drugs to children 4.6 million times. The most dangerous aspect of this is that most of these drugs have not been tested for safety for use by children. It is possible that drugs that are safe for adults may not be so safe for children.

The increased use of prescription drugs by children may be sending the wrong message that society accepts drug use. Teens who see their friends and parents take prescription drugs may get the idea that it's okay to solve their problems with drugs. They may also be more open to experimenting with illegal drugs.

There have been many documented

Prescribed drugs such as Valium, Xanax, and Prozac can cause violent behavior.

cases of suicide, assault, and homicide following psychiatric treatment that included these drugs.

A woman shot her two children only weeks after being released from a psychiatric ward. She had been treated with tranquilizers and antidepressants.

A young man committed suicide one month after withdrawal from Ritalin.

Scientific studies also show a connection between these psychiatric drugs and violence. A Canadian research team working with prisoners found that "violent, aggressive incidents occurred significantly more frequently in inmates when they were on psychiatric medication than when these inmates were not."

Other commonly prescribed drugs such as Valium, Xanax, and Prozac have been shown to cause violent behavior. As of 1992, more than 23,000 reports of adverse reactions to Prozac had been filed with the U.S. Food and Drug Administration, more than any other drug in the twenty-two-year history of the reporting system. This was in the first three and a half years the drug was on the market.

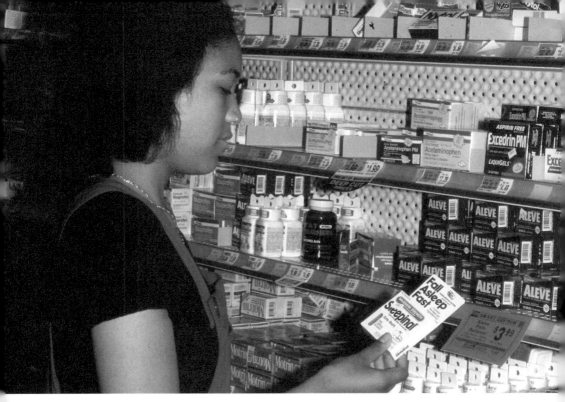

Any drug, whether legal or illegal, can be dangerous. You should use caution and common sense before taking any drug.

Not every mental-health professional agrees that these drugs are dangerous. Some believe that the psychosis was present before the drug treatment.

People should always be aware of how a drug, whether legal or illegal, can affect the user. Legal drugs can be as dangerous and addicting as illegal drugs. This chapter has shown how drugs, even those prescribed by doctors, can cause violence in users. Use caution and common sense before deciding to take *any* kind of drug.

Couriers who deliver drugs are not usually suspected
of carrying drugs because of their young age.

CHAPTER 4

The Business of Drugs

*T*he drug trade is international. Most of the drugs are grown in countries in the Middle East, South America, Central America, Mexico, and Cuba. They are smuggled by different routes into the United States, Canada, and Europe.

The drug business is structured like a legal corporation. The drug lord directs the growing, harvesting, and processing of the drugs. Drug lords have great power in their countries. They have armies of men who protect the crops from local police authorities.

The drug business has made Colombia one of the most violent countries in the world. Murders, kidnappings, disappearances, terrorist attacks, armed attacks,

and death threats are everyday occur- **41**
rences.

Money is the main reason for these violent crimes. Since the business is illegal, it is hard to say just how much money is involved. Some experts estimate that tens of billions of dollars are made each year. People will do anything to protect such large amounts of money. That's why the drug business is so dangerous.

Drug lords also use violence to intimidate and control people. The drug lord's armies shoot anyone who comes too close to the cultivated fields. Suspected spies for the local authorities are killed.

In Panama, the homicide rate has soared since 1990. From about 100 homicides a year in the 1980s, it climbed to 296 in 1991. In Venezuela, the number of weekend slayings tripled in four years. The primary factor in all those killings was the drug trade.

To protect their business, the drug lords also send hit teams to other countries to kill targeted people. It may be someone who is trying to take over a section of the business, or someone who is in jail on drug charges. By sending the hit team, the drug lord can eliminate the

42 | connection between himself and the drug business.

For many people in the drug business, such as gang members, it is an easy move from illegal drugs to other illegal actions. They are already operating outside the law, so murder is no problem. One member of New York's Vigilante gang stated it simply, "We sell drugs and we kill."

Many gangs exist simply to deal in drugs. This drug trade often leads to violence because gangs fight to maintain territory. Thousands of innocent people have died because they were caught in the cross fire of two rival gangs or were killed in a drive-by shooting.

A New Business

According to an article in *Parade* magazine (September 1994), the use of heroin is growing in the United States. In the 1980s its use was starting to decline as cocaine and crack had taken over as the drugs of choice among addicts. In recent years, however, a new kind of heroin, known as "China White," has become popular.

This heroin is purer than other forms of the drug and can be snorted or smoked. Experts believe that the risk of

Heroin is a very dangerous and addictive drug. It has ruined many lives including that of Kurt Cobain, lead singer of the grunge band, Nirvana. Cobain, a heroin user, committed suicide in 1994.

contracting AIDS from infected needles is what caused heroin use to decline. Now that needles are no longer necessary, more people are using the drug. As author Peter Maas wrote in the article, "The overdose death of the actor River Phoenix . . . and the suicide of the rock star Kurt Cobain, a heavy heroin user, appear to have had little impact."

Heroin is highly addictive. The longer it is used, the more it takes to achieve the same effect. One real danger to the user is the effort to withdraw. The symptoms include severe nausea and convulsions.

43

44   A particular danger of China White is its high potency. Some users move up from smoking and snorting heroin to injecting themselves with the drug, which can lead to a lethal overdose.

China White comes from the opium poppy fields in an area of Southeast Asia known as the Golden Triangle. The business is controlled by Chinese criminal societies called Triads, based in Hong Kong. The Triads smuggle the drugs into other countries. They often also control the sale of drugs from the highest level down to the streets.

China White hasn't been around long enough to impact studies of drugs and crime. But from what we know about the drug business, it is obvious that it can impact violence. The gangs controlling the cocaine and crack business do not want to lose out to the new guy with the new "product."

CHAPTER 5

Drugs on the Streets

In the last four years, Rosalyn Rice has seen forty friends killed by gunfire. Gang fights and drug violence are so common in her hometown that the city's murder rate is eight times that of the rest of the state.

Because death is so much a part of their daily lives, many of Rosalyn's classmates talk about their funerals the way some kids talk about their weddings. They plan what they will wear and who will be invited.

When Rosalyn first entered Central High, she started hanging out with known gang members. A friend, Terry, decided to watch over her. He warned her of the dangers on the streets.

One summer, while Rosalyn was away, Terry was killed. He had stopped a fight

Drugs have become a big business about making money.

*between his brother and rival gangs. A week
later he was shot at his front door.*

*Terry's death turned Rosalyn around. She
didn't want any part of the streets or the
gangs that ruled them. She only wished she
could have learned that without losing Terry.*

Rosalyn's story was written by
Geraldine Baum in *Seventeen* magazine
(June 1994). The real tragedy of the story is
that it could be told by many other people
across the country. Her story has a happy
ending in that Rosalyn was able to turn
her life around. Too many others don't.

Drugs have become a big business
about making money. Unfortunately, in

making money, drug dealers will do anything to protect their merchandise,
including murder. In every step that the
drugs take to get on the street, a profit is
made and the risk of violence is great.

Illegal drugs are brought into the
country by the "importer." They are sold
to the "supplier" or "main man." The
supplier sells the drugs to the "distributor," who then sells them to the "dealers."

The importer has to protect himself
against rivals. The supplier has to intimidate the distributor to make sure he turns
over the money once the drugs are sold.
Dealers are in constant danger from rival
gangs trying to move into their territory.

Once the drugs hit the streets, the
business is primarily controlled by gangs.
Some of the gangs are large and sophisti-
cated like the Asian Triads. Others are
smaller and loosely organized.

The dealer controls the sale of drugs in
a certain area or neighborhood. He may
use other gang members as lookouts,
spotters, and couriers. Others act as
enforcers or shotguns.

The youngest members are the lookouts
and spotters. Lookouts watch while a drug
deal is going on. Spotters direct custom-
ers to a house where they can buy drugs.

48 These jobs are particularly dangerous because the lookouts and spotters are so visible. They are often killed when rival gangs try to move in on the territory. They are also more likely to be arrested if the police show up.

Couriers deliver drugs. Because they are so young—usually under twelve—they are seldom suspected of carrying drugs. If a rival gang member knows they are on a delivery, however, they may be killed and robbed of the drugs.

Enforcers and shotguns protect the dealer and guard the whole operation from theft. They also keep out competition and collect debts. These are very dangerous roles. If an enforcer kills a rival gang member for trying to move into the territory, the enforcer is targeted for a revenge killing. Most enforcers end up seriously injured or dead in a few years.

From the drug lord to the youngest kid on the street, a chain of loyalty runs upward. The importer is loyal to the drug lord. The distributor is loyal to the importer. The dealer is loyal to the distributor. If anyone breaks the chain, he or she is killed.

Another common factor in all levels of the drug business is the need to be the

Dealers moving into small and rural areas establish a market by giving out free samples.

50 | "toughest guy around." Starting at the lowest level, you have to prove that you are tough enough to move up. You have to learn how to fight and how to intimidate others. In her book, *Violence and Drugs*, Gilda Berger reports on brutal and bizarre crimes committed by young dealers. In Detroit, boys as young as fourteen have been arrested for torture—using powerful electric shocks and pouring alcohol on open wounds.

Why Get Involved in Drugs?

A simple, one-word answer is money. People are drawn to the drug business by the lure of money, and the power and freedom it brings. They don't see the dangers—or they convince themselves that nothing could happen to them.

Some people also mistakenly believe they can be in the drug business without getting involved in the really dangerous stuff. They think they can just sell a few drugs, make a little money, and get out. The problem is that once they're in, there is no getting out.

The big guys in the business don't want anyone to talk to the police. They also don't want to lose anyone who is making money for them. A person who tries to leave is kept in line by threats and physical injury. If that doesn't work, he or she is killed.

As young teens move up in the business, they discover that the chain of loyalty doesn't go both ways. They have to be loyal to the person above them, but they can't trust that person. Everyone is constantly looking for ways to get ahead by getting rid of someone else.

The drug business has brought other dangers to the streets. Innocent people are often victims of drive-by shootings. They get caught in the cross fire between rival gangs. People high on drugs have brought violence to shopping malls, concerts, restaurants, and sporting events.

Drug dealers often introduce addicts to other crimes such as robbery, burglary, and prostitution. Dealers trade drugs for stolen property. They trade drugs for sex or sell an addict to someone else. Addicts who are willing to sell their bodies for drugs are referred to as "turned out." They get little or no respect in the business and are frequently abused.

Coming to Your Neighborhood
Until ten years ago, most of the drug and gang activity was in or around large cities.

52 | That is no longer true. Small towns and rural areas have become infected with drugs and all the crime and violence associated with them.

Violent crime in Nebraska rose dramatically from 1982 to 1992. Felony arrests rose 121 percent, murder grew 200 percent, and reported rapes grew 100 percent. An Omaha police officer reports that gang membership has grown from 300 members in the mid-1980s to more than 1,200 in 1994. He says that the growth is directly related to a surge in drug availability and use.

What is happening in Nebraska is happening in other midwestern states, small towns, and rural communities. Many big-city crack gangs have moved beyond their home bases. Los Angeles gangs have expanded to Kansas City, St. Louis, and Seattle. Miami gangs have turned up in Atlanta and Savannah.

The approach to a new city is organized and businesslike. The dealers pass out free samples to create a market. Then they recruit young addicts to work for them. Soon they have a growing business, with all the violence that goes with it.

Law enforcement agencies are setting up community centers to help keep kids away from drugs and gangs.

CHAPTER 6

Is It Hopeless?

The reality of drugs and violence paints a terrifying picture. Here, at the end of this book, we face the same questions we started with. When will it ever end? Or perhaps we even wonder *if* it will ever end.

The good news is that plenty of people are getting tired of the dangers and are taking action. Neighborhood groups are forming all across the country to take back their streets. Law-enforcement agencies are setting up community centers to direct kids away from drugs and gangs. Programs in schools are teaching kids about the dangers of drugs. They are also working to teach students how to resolve conflicts without pulling out a gun.

These efforts have made a difference, **55** and that is very encouraging.

A 1994 TV special titled "Victory over Violence" offered a great deal of hope. It featured more than thirty organizations or agencies tackling the problem in cities across the nation. The results were amazing. Just one example was Alma, Georgia, where a large part of the population lived in public housing.

In the 1980s, Alma was like a war zone. Drugs, gangs, and violence ruled the streets, and the housing projects were known as "Little Vietnam." In 1992, the police opened a substation in the middle of the projects.

At first, the people were against the station. They thought the police were there only to harass them. But the police officers worked to establish trust. They started an athletic league and a youth center. Young people were offered tutoring, social services, and vocational training. Most importantly, the young people had places to go to help keep them from getting involved with gangs and drugs.

In just one year the rate of juvenile crime dropped 68 percent. The people began to take pride in their community. Working with the police, they improved

56 their neighborhood and their lives.

Many experts believe that this is the best way to attack the problem of drugs and violent crime. One criminologist says, "We all have to take some responsibility for what is going on around us."

On a personal level, we can do a number of things. First and foremost, we can avoid adding to the problem by not taking drugs. We can even be brave enough to encourage our friends to be drug-free. It's easier to resist temptation when we share our efforts with someone else.

We can support neighborhood, school, church, or government efforts to fight the problem. Teenagers can be a vital part of neighborhood watch programs. They usually know more about what is happening in the area than anyone else.

It is important for each of us to develop a personal code of conduct. We can decide to do what is right simply because it is right. We can decide to do something to benefit others. We can decide to get involved with solutions and not be part of the problem.

Glossary
Explaining New Words

addiction   Constant need to use a drug.

amphetamines   Drugs that speed up the central nervous system.

barbiturates   Drugs that slow down or depress the central nervous system.

cocaine   Powerful stimulant made from the leaves of coca plants.

crack   Crystal form of cocaine, usually smoked.

crash   The effects when coming down from a drug high.

euphoria   A feeling of excitement or contentment.

hallucinogens   Drugs that make you see and hear things that aren't there.

heroin   White powder made from opium.

joint   Slang term for marijuana cigarette.

LSD   Drug that produces hallucinations.

methamphetamine   Stimulant with effects similar to cocaine.

morphine   Opiate used as a sedative and painkiller.

58 | **narcotics** Painkillers made from pop-
pies: opium, morphine, and heroin.

paranoid schizophrenia Mental disorder marked by delusions and sometimes hallucinations.

physical dependence Adaptation of
the body to the presence of a drug.

psychological dependence Condition
in which the drug user craves a drug
to maintain a sense of well-being.

psychosis Serious mental disorder
marked by partial or complete withdrawal from reality.

tolerance Decrease of physical reaction
to the effects of a drug.

Help List

HOT LINES

Covenant House Nine Line (800) 999-9999
International Institute on Inhalant Abuse (303) 788-1951
"Just Say No" Kids Club (800) 258-2766
Marijuana Anonymous (800) 766-6779
Nar-Anon (310) 547-5800
Narcotics Anonymous (818) 773-9999
National Institute on Drug Abuse (800) 662-HELP
National Runaway Switchboard (800) 621-4000
Youth Crisis Hot Line (800) 448-4663

Alcoholics Anonymous
P.O. Box 459
Grand Central Station
New York, NY 10163
(212) 870-3400
e-mail: 76245-2153@compuserv.com

National Black Alcoholism Council, Inc.
285 Gennesee Street
Utica, NY 13501
(314) 798-8066

National Clearinghouse for Alcohol and Drug Information
P.O. Box 2345
Rockville, MD 20847-2345
(301) 468-2600
web site: http://www.health.org
e-mail: info@prevline.health.org

60 | **National Council on Alcohol and Drug Dependence (NCADD)**
12 West 21st Street
New York, NY 10010
(212) 206-6770
(800) 622-2255
web site: http://www.ncadd.org
e-mail: national@NCADD.org

National Families in Action
2296 Henderson Mill Road
Atlanta, GA 30345
(770) 934-6364
web site: http://www.emory.edu/NFIA/

IN CANADA

Addictions Foundation of Manitoba
1031 Portage Avenue
Winnipeg, MB R3G OR8
(204) 944-6200

Alberta Alcohol and Drug Abuse Commission
2nd Floor, 10909 Jasper Avenue NW
Edmonton, AB T5J 3M9
(403) 427-4275
e-mail: AADAC@freenet.edmonton.ab.ca

Youth Detox Program
Family Services of Greater Vancouver
504 Cassiar Street
Vancouver, BC V5K 4M9
(604) 299-1131

For Further Reading

Adint, Victor. *Drugs and Crime*. New York: Rosen Publishing Group, 1994.

Berger, Gilda, and Berger, Melvin. *Drug Abuse A-Z*. Hillside, NJ: Enslow Publishing, Inc., 1990.

Brown, Gene. *Violence on America's Streets*. Brookfield, CT: Millbrook Press, 1992.

Campbell, Chris. *No Guarantees*. New York: Macmillan, 1993.

Condon, Judith. *The Pressure to Take Drugs*. New York: Franklin Watts, 1990.

Currie, Elliott. *Dope and Trouble*. New York: Pantheon Books, 1991.

———. *Reckoning: Drugs, the Cities, and the American Future*. New York: Hill and Wang, a division of Farrar, Straus and Giroux, 1993.

DeStafano, Susan. *Focus on Opiates*. Frederick, MD: Twenty-First Century Books, 1991.

Miller, Maryann. *Coping with Weapons and Violence in School and on Your Streets*. Rev. ed. New York: Rosen Publishing Group, 1996.

62 Peck, Rodney G. *Drugs and Sports*. New York: Rosen Publishing Group, 1992.

Rogak, Lisa. *Steroids: Dangerous Game*. Minneapolis: Lerner Publications, 1992.

Salak, John. *Drugs in Society*. New York: Twenty-First Century Books, 1993.

Seixas, Judith S. *Drugs: What They Are and What They Do*. New York: William Morrow & Co., 1991.

Shulman, Jeffrey. *Focus on Hallucinogens*. Frederick, MD: Twenty-First Century Books, 1991.

———. *The Drug-Alert Dictionary and Resource*. Frederick, MD: Twenty-First Century Books, 1991.

Smith, Judie. *Drugs and Suicide*. New York: Rosen Publishing Group, 1995.

Webb, Margot. *Coping with Street Gangs*. New York: Rosen Publishing Group, 1995.

Index

About the Author

Maryann Miller's work has been published in numerous magazines and Dallas newspapers. She has served as editor, columnists, reviewer, and feature writer. Currently she works as an office manager for a book distributor in Dallas.

Married for over twenty-nine years, Ms. Miller is the mother of five children. She and her husband live in Omaha, Nebraska.

Photo Credits

pp. 2, 26, 44 © A/P Wide World Photos; p. 8 by Yung-Hee Chia; p. 38 by Kim Sonsky; all other photos and cover by John Novajosky